Native American Library

AZTEC
History and Culture

Helen Dwyer and Mary Stout

Consultant Robert J. Conley
Sequoyah Distinguished Professor at Western Carolina University

Gareth Stevens
Publishing

Please visit our website, www.garethstevens.com. For a free color catalog of all our high-quality books, call toll free 1-800-542-2595 or fax 1-877-542-2596.

Library of Congress Cataloging-in-Publication Data

Dwyer, Helen
Aztec history and culture / Helen Dwyer and Mary A. Stout.
   p. cm. — (Native American library.)
Includes index.
ISBN 978-1-4339-7410-6 (paperback)
ISBN 978-1-4339-7411-3 (6-pack)
ISBN 978-1-4339-7409-0 (library binding)
1. Aztecs—Juvenile literature. I. Stout, Mary, 1954- II. Title.
F1219.73.D95 2013
972—dc23

                    2012002831

New edition published in 2013 by
Gareth Stevens Publishing
111 East 14th Street, Suite 349
New York, NY 10003

First edition published 2005 by Gareth Stevens Publishing

Copyright © 2013 Gareth Stevens Publishing

Produced by Discovery Books
Project editor: Helen Dwyer
Designer and page production: Sabine Beaupré
Photo researchers: Tom Humphrey and Helen Dwyer
Maps: Stefan Chabluk

Photo credits: Native Stock: pp. 36, 39 (bottom); Werner Forman Archive: pp. 10, 22, 23, 29; Bridgeman Art Library: pp. 11, 39 (top); Peter Newark's American Pictures: pp. 12, 15, 16, 17, 21 (both), 26, 27 (both), 35; Corbis: pp. 14, 20, 24, 25, 28, 30, 32 (Robert van der Hilst), 33 (Jazmin Adrián/Demotix); Courtesy of the Library of Congress: pp. 18, 19; Getty Images: p. 31 (AFP/Stringer); Shutterstock: pp. 5 (Sergei Chumakov), 34 (John Copeland); Wikimedia: pp. 6 (Jackhynes), 8, 37 (ALejandroLinaresGarcia), 38 (rosemania); p. 39 (top) (c) 2003 Banco de Mexico Diego Rivera & Frida Kahlo Museums Trust. Av. Cinco de Mayo No. 2, Del. Cuauhtemoc 06059, Mexico, D.F.

Printed in the United States of America

CPSIA compliance information: Batch #CS12GS: For further information contact Gareth Stevens, New York, New York at 1-800-542-2595.

CONTENTS

Introduction 4

Chapter 1: Land and Origins. 10

Chapter 2: History 12

Chapter 3: Traditional Way of Life 20

Chapter 4: Aztec Life Today. 30

Timeline 40

Glossary. 42

More Resources. 44

Things to Think About and Do 46

Index 47

Words that appear in the glossary are printed in **boldface** type the first time they appear in the text.

INTRODUCTION

Aztecs are a Native American people who lived in the Valley of Mexico from about eight hundred years ago. They are just one of the many groups of Native Americans who live today in the Americas. There are well over five hundred Native American tribes in the United States and more than six hundred in Canada. But who are Native Americans, and how do the Aztecs fit into the history of North America's native peoples?

THE FIRST IMMIGRANTS

Native Americans are people whose **ancestors** settled in North America thousands of years ago. These ancestors probably came from eastern parts of Asia. Their **migrations** probably occurred during cold periods called **ice ages**. At these times, sea levels were much lower than they are now. The area between northeastern Asia and Alaska was dry land, so it was possible to walk between the continents.

Scientists are not sure when these migrations took place, but it must have been more than twelve thousand years ago. Around that time, water levels rose and covered the land between Asia and the Americas.

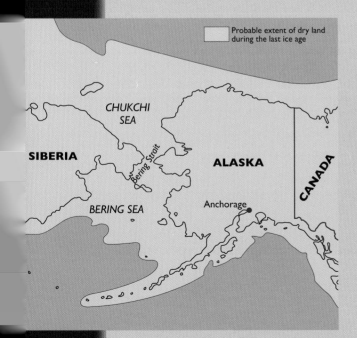

Probable extent of dry land during the last ice age

CHUKCHI SEA

SIBERIA

Bering Strait

ALASKA

CANADA

BERING SEA

Anchorage

Siberia (Asia) and Alaska (North America) are today separated by an area of ocean named the Bering Strait. During the last ice age, the green area on this map was at times dry land. The Asian ancestors of the Aztecs walked from one continent to the other.

The Cliff Palace at Mesa Verde, Colorado, is the most spectacular example of Native American culture that survives today. It consists of more than 150 rooms and pits built around A.D. 1200 from sandstone blocks.

By around ten thousand years ago, the climate had warmed and was similar to conditions today. The first peoples in North America moved around the continent in small groups, hunting wild animals and collecting a wide variety of plant foods. Gradually these groups spread out and lost contact with each other. They developed separate **cultures** and adopted lifestyles that suited their **environments.**

SETTLING DOWN

Although many tribes continued to gather food and hunt or fish, some Native Americans began to live in settlements and grow crops. Their homes ranged from underground pit houses and huts of mud and thatch to dwellings in cliffs. By 3500 B.C., a plentiful supply of fish in the Pacific Ocean and in rivers had enabled people to settle in large coastal villages from Alaska to Washington State. In the deserts of Arizona more than two thousand years later, farmers constructed hundreds of miles of **irrigation** canals to carry water to their crops.

The remains of the Avenue of the Dead and the Pyramid of the Sun at Teotihuacán. This city may have been home to 200,000 people.

In the Ohio River valley between 700 B.C. and A.D. 500, people of the Adena and Hopewell cultures built clusters of large burial mounds, such as the Serpent Mound in Ohio, which survives today. In the Mississippi **floodplains**, the native peoples formed complex societies. They created mud and thatch temples on top of flat earth pyramids. Their largest town, Cahokia, in Illinois, contained more than one hundred mounds and may have been home to thirty thousand people.

Meantime, in and around present-day Mexico, cities first appeared more than three thousand years ago. In the Valley of Mexico, the city of Teotihuacán dominated central Mexico and its **city-states** from around 100 B.C. to A.D. 600. During that time, it was one of the largest cities in the world. The people of Teotihuacán became wealthy through control of valuable trade routes and the development of advanced agriculture.

After the decline of Teotihuacán, Nahuatl-speaking peoples, including the ancestors of the Aztecs, moved south from northern Mexico, or possibly from the southwestern United States. By the thirteenth century, they were established in the Valley of Mexico. The Aztecs founded their city Tenochtitlán on an island in Lake Texcoco in 1325. Just over one hundred years later, the Aztecs were the most powerful people in the whole of Mexico.

CONTACT WITH EUROPEANS

Around A.D. 1500, European ships reached North and Central America. The first explorers were the Spanish. Armed with guns and riding horses, they took over land in present-day southeastern United States and Mexico and forced the Native Americans to work for them. The Spanish were followed by the British, Dutch, and French, who were looking for land to settle and for opportunities to trade.

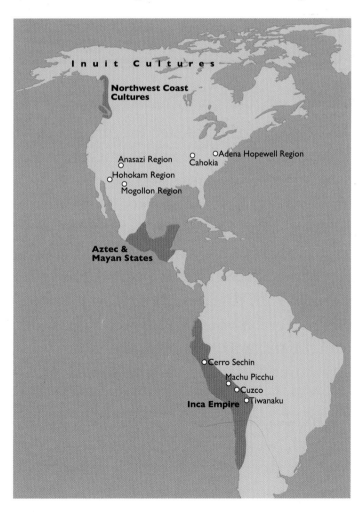

This map highlights some of the main early American cultures.

This illustration is from a book about Aztec history and culture that was compiled in the later sixteenth century. It shows an eagle warrior (left) and a jaguar warrior (right). Both are carrying war clubs with sharp blades.

The Spanish arrived in Mexico in 1519, and by 1522, they had conquered the Aztec Empire and destroyed Tenochtitlán. They immediately began to build Mexico City on the same site. Christian missionaries arrived soon after to convert and educate the Aztecs. They also worked to create a written form of the Nahuatl language, which eventually became an official language of the Spanish Empire in the Americas.

When Native Americans met Europeans they came into contact with diseases, such as **smallpox** and measles, that they had never experienced before. At least one half of all Native Americans, and possibly many more than that, were unable to overcome these diseases and died. In 1520, after the arrival of the Spanish, many Aztecs died in an outbreak of smallpox.

In Mexico, many Aztec people intermarried with the Spanish settlers. Most of the rest remained in country areas, which is where aspects of traditional life and the Nahuatl language continue today.

FIGHTING FOR SURVIVAL

Native Americans in the United States faced different problems. At the end of the 1700s, people of European descent began to migrate west, looking for new land to farm and exploit. Many Native Americans were forced onto **reservations**.

New laws in the United States and Canada took away most of the control Native Americans had over their lives. They were expected to adopt the ways and habits of white Americans. Native

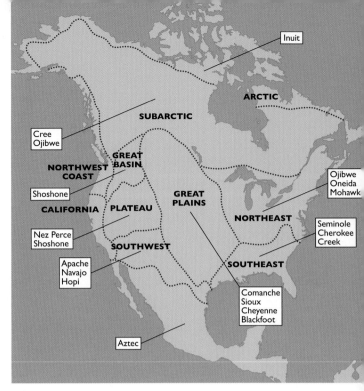

This map of North America highlights the main Native American cultural groups, along with the smaller groups, or tribes, featured in this series of books.

Americans on reservations endured poverty and very low standards of living. In the 1970s, the American Indian Movement (AIM) organized large protests that attracted attention worldwide and led to changes in U.S. policy. New laws protected Native American civil rights, and tribal governments were formed.

Like other Native Americans, the Nahua (Aztec) people in the twentieth century were poorer and lived in more rural areas than other ethnic groups. The survival of the Nahuatl language was severely threatened. In 1696, the Spanish tried to prevent people from speaking Nahuatl, and in 1770, use of the written language was also discouraged. Through most of the twentieth century, only Spanish was taught in schools. Then, in the 1990s, Mexican government policies toward native peoples improved. Today, Nahuatl is recognized as a national language in Mexico, and government agencies have been created to promote and protect native communities.

LAND AND ORIGINS

The red markings indicate the areas that the Aztecs conquered. Orange areas are independent territories.

LAND OF THE AZTECS

The Aztecs were an early Native American tribe who lived in central Mexico from about 1325 to 1521, when Spanish **conquistadors** destroyed them. Although the Aztecs don't exist as a tribe today, their **descendants** and those of other Nahuatl-speaking tribes from that time are known today as the Nahuas and number about 1.4 million.

AZTEC CREATION STORY

Like many ancient cultures, the Aztecs told an origin story that explained the history of the world. They believed that the earth was previously created and destroyed four times.

Quetzalcoatl and Tezcatlipoca, creators of the fifth world, found the earth covered with water, with only a giant monster living there. The gods tore the monster in two: the upper part of his body became land, and the lower part was thrown into the sky to become the stars. Two other gods, Nanaautzin and Tecuciztecatl, threw themselves into fire to

This beautiful mask represents one of the most powerful creator gods, Tezcatlipoca. He was called the "Smoking Mirror."

This page from an Aztec book shows the Aztecs leaving Aztlan to journey to their new home.

become the Sun and Moon. Quetzalcoatl then created humans by going to the underworld of the dead and gathering some old bones that he ground up and sprinkled with his own blood.

THE WANDERERS

The wandering Aztecs called themselves *Mexica* and began their journey at a place known as Aztlan. Because of the Mexicas' origins, other people called them "Aztecs." Leaving Aztlan as instructed by their god Huitzilopochtli, the Aztecs traveled for many years, looking for their new home, which they would recognize by a sign — an eagle perched on a cactus with a snake in its beak.

The Nahuatl Language

The Nahuatl language was spoken by the Aztecs and is still spoken today in the country of Mexico.

Nahuatl	Pronunciation	English
amatl	a-matl	codex
atl	a-tl	water
calli	kal-li	house
chocolatl	cho-ko-latl	chocolate
pilli	pil-li	noble person
pochtecatl	poch-te-katl	merchant
telpochcalli	tel-poch-kal-li	school, college
teocalli	te-o-kal-li	temple

HISTORY

Chapter 2

THE RISE OF THE AZTECS

In 1168, the Aztecs came to the Valley of Mexico, which was already home to many other people. These people were descendants of the Toltecs, an advanced warrior society that ruled Mexico from the tenth to the twelfth centuries. The Aztecs claimed descent from the Chichimecs, a wild, wandering, and warlike people.

Eventually, the Aztecs settled near the Culhuas, who ruled them. The warlike Aztecs became hired soldiers who helped the Culhuas defeat neighboring tribes in battle. A grateful Culhua chief gave his daughter to the Aztec chief to marry, but instead she was **sacrificed** to their god Huitzilopochtli, which angered the Culhuas. War broke out between the Culhuas and the Aztecs, and the Aztecs fled to a swampy island in the middle of Lake Texcoco. Here, the Aztecs saw an eagle perched on a cactus with a snake in its mouth, just as their god had predicted. They began building their new home on the island in 1325. They named the city Tenochtitlán.

The first page of the *Codex Mendoza*, a book written by an unknown Aztec artist for the first Spanish governor of New Spain, tells the story of the Aztecs settling in Tenochtitlán. It is also a map of this island city-state.

Tenochtitlán was on an island in the middle of Lake Texcoco, reached only by four causeways (raised roads through water). Canals (shown in blue) crisscross the island. The Axayacatl Palace, originally where an earlier Aztec ruler lived, became the guest house for the Spanish army when Emperor Motecuhzoma (also spelled Montezuma) first welcomed them to Tenochtitlán.

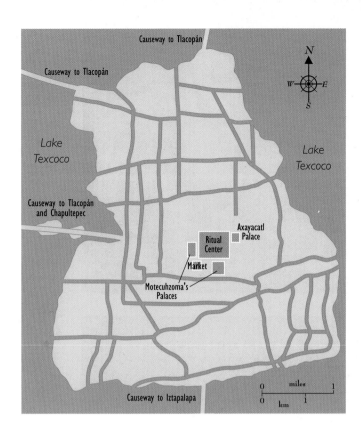

THE AZTEC EMPIRE

The Aztecs became stronger and more powerful on their island city, and their warriors began to conquer neighboring tribes. During the mid-1400s, an agreement with two other city-states created the ruling Triple **Alliance**, made up of Tenochtitlán, Texcoco, and Tlacopán. These three city-states ruled over 12 million people in the Valley of Mexico. Though required

Chinampas

The chinampas, or "floating gardens," were the Aztecs' clever solution to the problem of how to expand a city that was on an island in the middle of a lake. First, they wove reeds together to form a raft-like base. Then they brought soil by canoe from the mainland to put on the reeds. Built in shallow water near shore, chinampas were held in place by posts sunk into the lake bed and by the roots of trees and plants. The Aztecs planted food crops and built thatched houses on the chinampas.

An Aztec sculpture. Aztec warriors were skillful and fierce — but they didn't try to kill their enemies. Their main job was to capture prisoners and conquer new lands so their people would pay tribute to the Aztecs.

Paying Tribute to the Aztecs

One Aztec book, the *Codex Mendoza*, records the tribute sent to the Aztecs by various people. The twice-yearly tribute of the province of Xoconosco consisted of:

2 jade necklaces

2,400 bundles of colored feathers

160 pelts of blue cotingas (birds)

800 bundles of yellow feathers

800 bundles of long quetzal (bird) tail feathers

2 lip plugs made of amber and gold

200 loads of cocoa beans

40 jaguar skins

800 gourd bowls

2 bricks of amber

to pay **tribute** to the Triple Alliance, the conquered people were left alone. They had to send bird feathers (highly valued for majestic cloaks and headdresses), food, jewelry, cocoa beans, slaves, and other valuables to Tenochtitlán twice a year. Many of the conquered people were unhappy with their rulers since they had to pay such huge tributes.

THE SPANISH CONQUEST

In 1519, Hernán Cortés, a Spanish conquistador, arrived in Mexico. He was searching for gold, but he also wanted to win lands for the Spanish kingdom and souls for his Catholic religion. Motecuhzoma II, the Aztec emperor, knew of Cortés's arrival from his spies. Though Motecuhzoma refused his requests to visit the capital city, Cortés decided to march to Tenochtitlán anyway. On his way, he passed through the lands of the Totonacs, who joined the Spanish conquistadors and encouraged Cortés to defeat the Aztecs.

La Malinche

A young native woman helped Hernán Cortés conquer Tenochtitlán. Malintzin (also called Dona Marina or La Malinche) was one of the slaves given to Cortés after he defeated a coastal tribe. Only fourteen years old, she spoke both Maya and Nahuatl and quickly learned Spanish. With Malintzin at his side translating, Cortés could communicate with the people of the Aztec Empire. She helped Cortés convince other tribes to join the Spanish to defeat the Aztecs. While many Native Americans respected her power, others disliked her for helping the Spanish take over Mexico. Today, Mexicans still use "La Malinche" to refer to a traitor.

Cortés and his army of five hundred men came to Mexico by ship from Cuba, another Spanish colony. Cortés's men were afraid of the native people and wanted to return, so Cortés burned his own boats. His men had no choice but to follow him as he marched on and destroyed Tenochtitlán.

GUESTS TAKE A PRISONER

Since he had no choice, Motecuhzoma at last invited Cortés to come to Tenochtitlán, treating the Spaniards as honored guests. In return, however, Cortés took the emperor prisoner. Motecuhzoma's brother, Cuitlahuac, led the Aztec warriors against the Spanish conquistadors and drove them out of Tenochtitlán in a fierce battle that ended with two-thirds of the conquistadors dead. During the battle, Motecuhzoma was also killed. While Cortés planned a new attack on Tenochtitlán, Cuitlahuac became the new emperor.

And the fighting men were all very well armed and bedecked with feathers, white, red, yellow, blue, green, black, and every color, all with different plumes on their heads and backs; round their necks they wore many jewels of gold, set with stones, as well as bracelets of brilliant gold . . .

Spanish priest Fray Duran describing Aztec noble warriors setting out to conquer another tribe

The Spanish conquest of Mexico as portrayed in an Aztec book of pictures. The Native Americans were amazed and frightened by the ships, horses, and guns owned by the Spanish.

Motecuhzoma II

Motecuhzoma II became the Aztec emperor in 1502, when he was about thirty-three years old. Although he was a respected warrior, he showed uncertainty in dealing with Cortés and the Spaniards. Cortés told Motecuhzoma he was a friendly **ambassador** from Spain, and the king of Texcoco advised Motecuhzoma to treat the Spaniards as friends. However, Motecuhzoma's brother and his cousin thought that Cortés was an enemy invader who should be attacked. Other advisors suggested that Cortés might be a returning god.

After Cortés imprisoned him in his own palace, Motecuhzoma stood on his roof and asked his people to stop fighting when they rose up against the Spanish invaders. They ignored him, and Motecuhzoma was killed in the battle that took place. No one knows for sure whether he was killed by the Spanish or the Aztecs.

Although the Spaniards did not plan on it, they brought another threat to the Aztecs in the form of a deadly disease — smallpox — to which the natives had no **immunity**. A smallpox **epidemic** broke out, killing many Aztecs, including the new emperor. In 1521, a young man called Cuauhtemoc, the last Aztec emperor, prepared for Cortés's attack. After seventy-five days of fierce battles in the city, the Spanish triumphed, and the Aztecs surrendered.

AFTER THE CONQUEST

After the Aztecs surrendered to the Spanish, their Native American enemies continued to kill the Aztecs and destroy Tenochtitlán. One source listed the death toll at 117,000 people. The city lay in ruins; many survivors left to settle elsewhere. After putting Emperor Cuauhtemoc in prison, the conquistadors made slaves of the surviving Aztec warriors.

An Aztec illustration shows the Spanish killing Motecuhzoma and dumping his body into a Tenochtitlán canal. The Spanish books say that the Aztecs killed their own emperor by throwing stones at him. Motecuhzoma's death remains a mystery to this day.

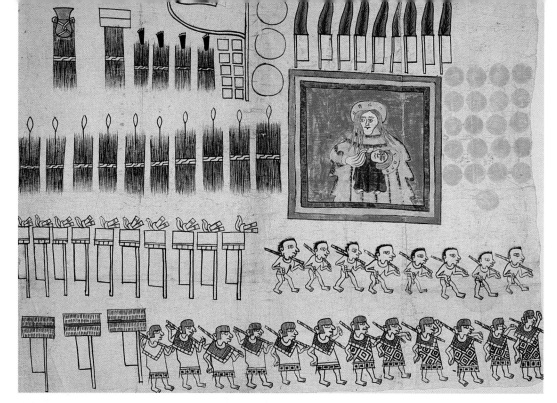

After the Spanish conquered the Aztecs, the native people still paid tribute — this time to the Spanish instead of Motecuhzoma. This record of the tribute paid in 1531 is written in the same manner that the Aztecs always kept their records.

Let me tell you about the dead bodies. I swear that all the houses on the lake were full of heads and corpses. . . . The streets, squares, houses, and courts were filled with bodies so that it was almost impossible to pass. Even Cortés was sick.

Bernal Diaz del Castillo, a Spaniard who traveled with Cortés, writing about Tenochtitlán after the Aztec defeat

To reward his men, Cortés set up a system of *encomiendas,* giving them large areas of land and native slaves to work it. He rebuilt the city of Tenochtitlán, calling it Mexico City after the Mexican people. It still bears that name today. Other changes followed: settlers were encouraged to come from Spain, Aztec schools were closed, and Christian schools were opened.

Diseases brought by the Spanish continued to kill the Native American people. Although 25 million Native American people lived in Mexico when the Spanish arrived, by 1592, the population had dropped to less than 2 million.

A MIX OF CULTURES

Mexico City became the capital of a Spanish colony called New Spain, and boatloads of Spanish people continued to come and settle in the new land, growing sugarcane and mining silver. The native people became a part of the lower **class** of the **colonial** society, working for the Spanish. The Spanish brought the Catholic religion, and many Native Americans became Catholic and were educated in Christian schools. The two cultures began to blend together, a process that continued for over two hundred years.

When Mexico became independent of Spain in 1821, the people began to look at their Aztec heritage with pride. Their heritage showed in the new Mexican national flag, which represented the Aztec story — an eagle perched on a cactus with a snake in its mouth. The descendants of all of the different Native American tribes living in the Valley of Mexico became known as Nahuas since they all spoke Nahuatl. By the 1910 Mexican Revolution, most Nahuas also had Spanish ancestors, because of the many marriages between Spanish and natives in the past. Today, Mexican culture is a mixture of Spanish, Aztec, and other native heritages.

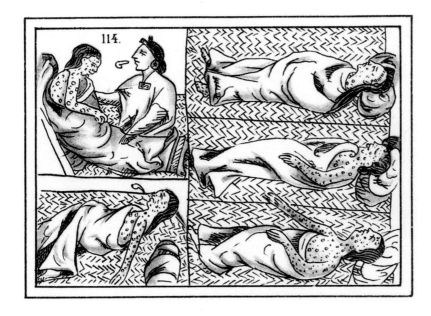

Thousands of Aztecs died from smallpox itself, and more died from hunger. So many people were ill that there was no one left to care for them. Today, people wonder if the Aztecs might have defeated the Spanish had they not been so sick with smallpox.

TRADITIONAL WAY OF LIFE

In Aztec society, clothing was based on social class. Only nobles wore clothes made of cotton with bright colors, rich decorations, and feathers.

AZTEC SOCIETY

Aztec society was highly organized, and each person knew his or her place in it from birth. At the top were the nobles, who owned the land, ran the government, and were in charge of the army. Because they spoke with the gods and acted as leaders, priests were also important in Aztec society. The Aztec middle class was made up of merchants and highly skilled **artisans**, such as the feather workers and stonemasons. The commoners, or lower class, were farmers, soldiers, and laborers.

The lowest class was made up of slaves. While some slaves were captured in war, sometimes Aztecs sold themselves into slavery if they couldn't make a living. If a commoner didn't pay his taxes, he could become a slave. If he became a successful soldier or priest, however, he could become one of the lower class of nobles; all the highest nobles were born into their class.

All the people, except for the nobles, were expected to pay a tax or contribute labor to the nobles.

This life-size carving of an Aztec eagle warrior shows him wearing the feathered helmet shaped like an eagle's head with its mouth open.

Aztec Warriors

The Aztecs battled neighboring peoples to take captives, who were then offered for sacrifice at the top of the temple steps in Tenochtitlán. Although human sacrifice to the gods existed in other cultures, the thirsty Aztec gods required much more blood than others.

Important people in Aztec society, warriors could be from the noble or lower classes. As in today's military, their dress reflected their rank. A warrior who took one captive in war without help carried an oak club and a plain shield and wore a cloak decorated with flowers. A two-captive warrior could wear sandals, a cone-shaped hat, and a feathered suit. The four-captive warrior was allowed to wear an outfit made with jaguar skin. Known as "eagle warriors," the top warriors wore eagle feathers and helmets shaped like eagle heads.

The artisans gave the nobles feather cloaks, **obsidian** blades, ceramic figures, or other products of their work. Farmers contributed food and labor; for example, their wives might weave for the nobles for several weeks each year.

FIRST A THIEF, THEN A SLAVE

The organized Aztecs also had a legal system with many judges and courts. Nobles and commoners went to different courts. Aztec records show more than eighty crimes listed with punishments. The most serious crimes were theft, murder, and public drunkenness. As a punishment for stealing, a thief was made a slave to the person from whom he or she stole.

CHILDHOOD AND MARRIAGE

Children were important to all Aztecs, nobles and commoners alike. Four days after birth, a **midwife** took the Aztec child outside for a **ritual** bath, and symbols of the baby's life were placed in its hands. For example, a boy baby might be given a little shield and arrow. When children were three years old, they began to be taught by their parents how to help and were given small tasks. Sometime between the ages of seven and fourteen, the children were sent to school. All Aztec children attended school, but there were different schools for nobles and commoners.

Sculpture of a girl. When an Aztec baby girl was given her first ritual bath, symbols of her future life, such as a little red basket and a weaver's tools, were placed in her hands.

Girls were ready for marriage at age fifteen or later, and boys were usually ready when they finished school at age twenty. Following the selection of a lucky wedding day according to the Aztec calendar, a large celebration and feast were prepared. At the end of the first day, the bride and groom sat on a mat in front of a fire. Their **matchmaker** tied the ends of the bride's and groom's new capes together, and they were married. Often, the wedding party continued for a week.

CLASS AFFECTS HOUSING AND CLOTHING

Aztec homes were different depending upon the class of the owner. Nobles lived in large two-story homes with many rooms, made with stone walls and log-and-plaster roofs, while commoners lived in huts made from **adobe** bricks with thatched roofs.

The clothing worn by the Aztecs was also based on their social class. Only nobles wore capes made of beautiful bird feathers and jewelry of gold and turquoise or jade stones. Excellent weavers,

Most Aztec households used bowls and drinking cups made from clay. These beautifully designed cups were used by a noble household. Noble homes also held clay figurines and decorations.

Aztec Games: Better Not Lose . . .

The Aztecs enjoyed games, including *patolli*, a board game like backgammon, and a ball game called *tlachtli*, which was also played by the Mayans and other Central American peoples. Two teams of two or three people played tlachtli on a court shaped like a capital "I." Stone rings were attached 27 feet (8 meters) high on each side of the court. Players put on padded knee, arm, and hip protectors and tried to knock the hard rubber ball through the rings, mostly with their hips. This game also had religious connections, as the ball represented the Sun and Moon, and the ball court was the world. The Aztecs believed that the outcome of a ball game could sometimes foretell the future, and nobles would often bet on the game. At times, the losing team would be sacrificed.

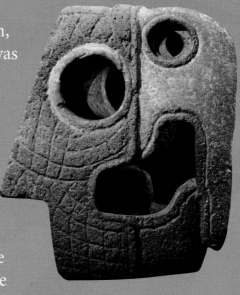

Shaped like the head of a macaw bird, this ball-game marker is from one of the ancient tlachtli ball courts. Although we know stone markers were placed on the ground in the ball courts, no one is sure how they were used during the game.

Aztec women used the fibers from cotton, maguey (agave), and hemp plants to make cloth. Women usually wore skirts and *huipiles* (a type of blouse), and men wore loincloths and capes.

Aztecs grew a variety of food crops, including corn, beans, onions, peppers, tomatoes, squash, and fruit. They also ate fish, ducks, and turkeys. Only nobles were allowed to hunt larger animals. One favorite Aztec food was **tamales**, which the bride and groom ate as part of their wedding ceremony.

THE ARTS

The Aztecs believed that art was a reflection of and communication with the gods. Their culture was richly artistic, and the style of their art was rooted in the Toltec culture. The Aztecs deeply appreciated speeches and poetry, some of which survive, like this poem about Tenochtitlán:

The city is spread out in circles of jade,
Radiating flashes of light like quetzal plumes.
Beside it lords are borne in boats:
Over them extends a flowery mist.

Their sculptors carved calendars, gods, goddesses, and animals from stone and created beautiful mosaics from precious stones. Jewelers made intricate jewelry from gold and precious stones. However, the most valued art form was feather work. Skilled artisans created amazing headdresses and capes from the brightly colored feathers of tropical birds, such as the quetzal, parrot, macaw, and hummingbird, for the nobles to wear.

There is one square . . . where are daily assembled more than sixty thousand souls, engaged in buying and selling; and where are found all kinds of **merchandise** . . . for instance articles of food, as well as jewels of gold and silver, lead, brass, copper, tin, precious stones, bones, shells, snails, and feathers.

Hernán Cortés describing the Aztec markets to King Charles of Spain

The Aztecs actually had two calendar systems to keep track of days. Weighing 25 tons (23 metric tons) and measuring 12 feet (3.6 m) in diameter, this stone shows the symbols for the Aztec months but does not actually function as a working calendar. The Sun god is in the center of the stone, which shows the four previous worlds.

Codices: Aztec Picture Books

The Aztecs used a picture-based writing system to create painted books called codices (singular: codex). They folded deerskin or paper made from bark to form books. Then, painters made dyes from ashes and plants and painted their stories on the codices. For example, a picture of a shield and arrows meant war, and one of footprints told of a journey. The painted symbol for Tenochtitlán was a picture of a cactus on a rock. Not only were Aztec codices full of information, but they were beautiful works of art as well.

After the conquest, the Spanish tried to destroy all the codices and replace them with their own writing system and their own books. Fifteen codices still exist today, however; we can read them to find out about the Aztecs from their own writings.

This picture from the Florentine Codex shows Aztec goldsmiths at work.

Quetzalcoatl, whose name means "Feathered Serpent," was one of the most important gods of ancient Mexico. Originally worshipped by the Toltecs, Quetzalcoatl was also honored by the Aztecs as a one of the creators of the world.

RELIGIOUS BELIEFS

The Aztecs had too many gods to count: one **source** says over sixteen hundred. As the Aztecs expanded their empire and conquered other tribes, they also included the conquered tribes' gods with their own. Some gods were considered more important than others, however; in fact, the Great Pyramid of Tenochtitlán, in the center of the city, contains only two temples. One is the sacred space for Huitzilopochtli, the Aztecs' ancestor god of the Sun, war, and sacrifice. The other is for Tlaloc, the god of rain. While war was important in Aztec society, rain was crucial for crops to grow.

The chief god of the fifth world in which the Aztecs lived was Tonatiuh, the old Sun god. Quetzalcoatl, a special helper to the Aztec priests, was a god of creation and the wind. The Aztecs believed that someday, earthquakes would destroy this world and sky monsters would eat the people.

Connected with fate, both good and bad, Tezcatlipoca was important to Aztec rulers, who often prayed to this god known as "Night Wind."

Human Sacrifice

The Aztecs believed that it was the task of humans to sacrifice themselves to keep the Sun moving and the world going. The Sun god fought a daily battle in the sky; human blood was a necessary food for the Sun to continue rising.

Sacrifices were only carried out as religious rituals by priests in temples. The type of sacrifice depended upon which god was being honored. Humans sacrificed to the rain god were drowned; victims of other sacrifices might be shot with arrows or dropped from a high place. To honor Huitzilopochtli, the hearts of enemy captives were cut out with sharp obsidian-blade knives and offered, still beating, to the Sun. The Aztecs honored the victims of the sacrifices, usually enemy warriors, and treated them like gods before their sacrifice. They were assured of a place in heaven.

An Aztec priest, wearing a white cape, performs a ritual human sacrifice to honor and feed the gods.

GODS AND SOULS

According to the Aztec creation story, when this world was created, two gods volunteered to sacrifice themselves to become the Sun and Moon. Once created, however, the Sun didn't move in the sky until two more gods were sacrificed. Quetzalcoatl, creator of the fifth world, cut open their chests and offered their hearts to Tonatiuh, the Sun god.

The Aztecs believed that each person had three souls. The cause of a person's death determined how long their three souls would travel. The souls of people who died ordinary deaths took a four-year journey to the underworld, and they were buried or **cremated** with tools and weapons to help them on their travels. People who were sacrificed or killed in war went to various places in the heavens, and their souls only took eighty days to reach their destination.

Another Aztec god, Xipe Totoc ("Our Flayed Lord") was an agricultural god of seeds and **fertility**. Here, he is shown wearing the skin of a human sacrifice to represent seeds bursting from their skins to grow.

AZTEC LIFE TODAY

The Nahuas Today

The modern Nahuas are Indians who are descended from the Nahuatl-speaking tribes that lived in the Valley of Mexico during the 1500s, including the Aztecs of Tenochtitlán, as well as natives from other city-states. Over the years, marriage between the Spaniards and Nahuas has resulted in a new Mexican culture that has borrowed elements from both cultures.

This Nahua woman and her daughter are descendants of the ancient Nahuatl-speaking tribes in Mexico. Today, more than one million Nahuas still speak Nahuatl, the language of the ancient Aztecs.

The Aztec Culture in Danger

Most Indians became Christians after the Spanish conquest, worshipping in churches built in the same places where Aztec temples had been torn down. The native people no longer practiced human sacrifice, their government was destroyed, and their trade and tribute economy was replaced.

A Pipil dancer takes part in the World Day of Indigenous Peoples in El Salvador in 2010. Pipils are Nahuatl speakers in Guatemala, El Salvador, and Honduras. They were Nahuas who left Mexico before the Spanish conquerors arrived.

THE AZTEC LANGUAGE

The most important surviving element of Nahua culture is the Nahuatl language, which is still spoken today by around one and a half million people, mainly in the countryside. Around 200,000 of these people speak no other language. Many of them survive by farming to feed themselves. If they work for other people, they earn less than the minimum wage. They tend to have spent less time in schools and have less education than other Mexicans. Only two-thirds of Nahuatl speakers can read and write the language.

Most Nahuatl speakers live in the states of Guerrero and Hidalgo, but they can be found in small numbers from the north to the southeast of the country. A few Mexican communities in New York and California also speak Nahuatl.

A teacher of Nahuatl (right) offers language courses in Mexico City. The written language uses the same letters as Spanish because it was first written down by Spanish priests.

In the twentieth century, Mexican schools taught only in Spanish and discouraged all native languages. This changed in 2003, when new laws recognized all Mexico's native languages as national languages that can be used in homes, workplaces, and schools. In 2008, the mayor of Mexico City campaigned to teach Nahuatl to all government employees.

FINDING WORK

The problems that Nahuas face today are the same as those experienced by many Native Americans. They are poor and live in rural areas without enough hospitals or schools. They don't have good jobs unless they move to the cities, and there isn't much for young people to do. Many men, young and old, move away from their home areas to join the army, work on cattle ranches and plantations, or move to the crowded **slums** surrounding the cities, in the hope of finding work in factories.

NAHUA HOMES

Indian peasant communities continued to build adobe houses and make and use household goods and tools much as the Aztecs did.

Today, many country people still live in simple one-room houses with earth floors. Inside are fireplaces surrounded by large stones on which cooking pots are placed. A small, high table serves as an altar and holds religious items, such as a cross, candles, and pictures of saints. Woven mats are stored around the walls during the day. They are opened up at night and used as mattresses to sleep on.

Around each house is a garden where useful plants are tended and small animals such as turkeys and ducks are kept. Further away are farming plots where crops are grown. The foods the Nahuas grow — corn, beans, tomatoes, chilies, and squashes — are the same as Aztec foods. Fish caught in local streams and rivers are a useful extra source of food.

Today in many places, modern homes are being built for the Nahuas, and some villages now have electricity and running water.

RELIGIOUS BELIEFS

Nahua religion is usually a mixture of Spanish Catholic ideas and their own native beliefs. The Nahuas pray to many earth, water, and heavenly spirits when they need help. For example, when they need more rain to make their crops grow well, they may ask a water or heavenly spirit to help them.

This traditional dance, which takes place at religious festivals, is performed to drive away wild animals that destroy crops and kill domestic animals.

A few Nahuas are traditional priests who receive guidance from dreams or make contact with the spirits. They are also healers. For example, some set broken bones, while others treat illnesses with plant medicines.

The Nahuas also take part in religious ceremonies, especially at times when crops are planted and harvested.

The Volador Dance

Aztec influence is strongly felt in dances and celebrations. Today, one can still see the volador, an Aztec dance that was probably originally created to ask the gods to end a terrible **drought**. In this dance, four men dressed as colorful birds are attached by ropes to a tall pole. They swing around and around as they are lowered to the ground. A fifth man stands on top of the pole, dancing and playing a flute and a drum.

Men from Veracruz state take part in a performance of the volador dance.

The Virgin of Guadalupe

The Virgin of Guadalupe remains an important religious figure for Mexicans. On December 12 each year, millions gather in churches all over the country to pray, celebrate, and honor La Reina de México (the Queen of Mexico).

When the Spanish first introduced the god of their Christian religion, the Aztecs welcomed the new Christian god and saints as they had the gods of all their enemies. Over the years, the Nahuas connected some Christian saints with the Aztec traditional gods.

In Mexico today, the Virgin of Guadalupe is a very important religious figure. She is a brown-skinned Mother of God who appeared in 1531 to Juan Diego, a poor Nahua man, and spoke to him in Nahuatl, saying she would protect native people. This event happened in a place sacred to the Aztec mother goddess Tonantzin, and many experts think that the Virgin of Guadalupe is a blend of the Virgin Mary and Tonantzin.

Modern-day descendants of the Aztecs, members of the Efigenio family dress in traditional clothing of the noble class.

TRADITIONAL CLOTHING

In some villages today, women continue to spin thread by hand and weave it on a back-strap loom that is similar to the looms used by Aztec women. As well as weaving cotton and wool for their clothing, the Nahuas weave maguey fibers to make bags and sacks.

Many Nahuas wear traditional clothing. The women's costumes are quite elaborate: short-sleeved, white blouses with embroidered decorations; colorful skirts, with embroidered underskirts for special occasions; small ponchos or capes over the blouses; and, as a top layer, dark-colored scarves or shawls. Men who still prefer traditional clothing wear cotton shirts and pants with woolen overshirts.

Day of the Dead

One of the most important Mexican celebrations today is called Dia de los Muertos, or Day of the Dead. During the celebration, which usually occurs during a week at the end of October and beginning of November, ancestors are honored in ceremonies that have many Aztec elements. Mexicans create an altar honoring dead family member(s) and place food and **incense** on it as an offering, just as the Aztecs did. The decorations on the altars often include skulls — a popular Aztec image — made of sugar. It is believed that the spirits of the dead return to the earth to connect with their living family members for a short period of time, then return to the grave.

Crowds celebrating the Day of the Dead in the Zócalo, Mexico City, carry a model called the Tree of Death. It portrays Mictlantecuhtli, the Aztec god of the dead.

The National Museum of Anthropology in Mexico City displays a model of the important buildings that once stood in the center of the Aztec city of Tenochtitlán.

CONTEMPORARY AZTEC INFLUENCE

Although the Aztec civilization no longer exists as it did in the 1500s, modern Mexican culture reflects its Aztec heritage and spirit. Spanish, the main language of Mexico, uses many Aztec words, such as *tomate*, *chocolat*, and *tamale*.

Aztec temples are now museums and contain Aztec art. For example, the Templo Mayor Museum in Mexico City is close to what remains of the Aztec temple, and it contains archaeological finds from the site. The National Museum of **Anthropology**, also in Mexico City, contains many famous Aztec objects. The careful preservation and study of their Aztec history reflects the pride Mexicans have in their heritage.

Twentieth-century Mexican artists such as Diego Rivera (1886–1957) created colorful murals containing Aztec symbols, faces, and scenes. Rivera's best-known works of this sort are murals of Aztec life in Tenochtitlán, which are located in the National Palace in Mexico City.

Proud of his country's Aztec heritage, Mexican artist Diego Rivera often featured Mexico's early history in his murals. This 1950 mural, *The Culture of Totonaken*, shows the nobles of the Totonac city-state visiting the market in Tenochtitlán to trade with the Aztecs.

Large Mexican marketplaces still sell traditional Aztec crafts such as woven cloth, carved wood, and pottery. Since the 1960s, many Nahuas in Guerrero state have been producing paintings of rural scenes on amate bark paper, the traditional paper used by the Aztecs. These paintings are popular in city markets with tourists and with collectors worldwide. The Aztecs continue to live on in many aspects of current Mexican culture.

Markets featuring colorful arts and crafts of Aztec design can be found in many places in Mexico today.

TIMELINE

between 500s and 1100s	Ancestors of the Aztecs arrive in Mexico from the north and move around, looking for areas to settle.
1168	Aztecs wander into the Valley of Mexico.
1325	Aztecs flee to an island and begin building Tenochtitlán.
1376	First Aztec emperor chosen.
about 1430	The Triple Alliance is formed between three city-states: Tenochtitlán, Texcoco, and Tlacopán.
1440	Motecuhzoma I begins his rule as fifth emperor of the Aztecs; Aztec civilization is at its peak, dominating the Valley of Mexico and the Gulf of Mexico.
1450s	Flooding and famine in Tenochtitlán.
1502	Motecuhzoma II becomes emperor of the Aztecs.
1517	Aztecs believe the appearance of a comet warns of a great disaster.
1519	The population of Mexico is 25 million native people; Hernán Cortés arrives in Mexico.
1520	Cortés allies with the Tlaxcala people, enemies of the Aztecs; Aztecs defeat Cortés, who is forced to retreat; smallpox epidemic strikes the Aztecs.
1521	The Aztecs surrender to the Spanish conquistadors; Tenochtitlán is destroyed.
1522	Building of Mexico City begins on the Tenochtitlán site.

1525	Cuauhtemoc, the last Aztec emperor, is killed by the Spanish; Cortés named governor-general of New Spain (Mexico).
1530s and 1540s	Spanish missionaries introduce schools for the Aztecs and teach them European languages; they also promote the writing of the Nahuatl language.
1531	The Virgin of Guadalupe appears to Juan Diego.
1540s	Severe smallpox epidemic among the Aztecs kills many people.
1547	The first Nahuatl grammar is published.
1570s	Severe typhus epidemic kills many Aztecs.
1570	Nahuatl becomes the official language of the Spanish empire in the Americas.
1592	The native population of Mexico drops to less than two million.
1696	Nahuatl language is banned in the Spanish empire.
1821	Mexico gains independence from Spain; renewal of interest in Aztec heritage.
1895	Five percent of Mexicans still speak Nahuatl.
2003	Mexican law recognizes the right of Mexicans to speak Nahuatl and other native languages at all times.
2008	Mayor of Mexico City campaigns to teach Nahuatl to all goverment employees.
2011	More than one million Mexicans speak Nahuatl; for nearly 200,000 of them, it is the only language they speak.

GLOSSARY

adobe: a building material made of mud mixed with straw.

alliance: an agreement among two or more groups to work together on a common goal.

ambassador: someone who represents or speaks for their own country while in a foreign country.

ancestors: people from whom an individual or group is descended.

anthropology: the study of human societies.

artisan: a skilled worker who makes things by hand.

city-states: large cities and the area surrounding each that are independent and have their own rulers.

class: divisions of society into social groups that are alike in some way. A society is often divided into upper, middle, and lower classes.

codex: a handwritten book made of picture symbols painted on paper. The plural of *codex* is *codices*.

colonial: relating to a colony, an area controlled by another nation.

conquistadors: Spanish conquerors.

cremated: disposed of by burning to ashes.

culture: arts, beliefs, and customs that make up a people's way of life.

descendants: all the children and children's children of an individual or group; those who come after.

drought: a long period with no rainfall.

environment: objects and conditions all around that affect living things and communities.

epidemic: a sudden increase of a rapidly spreading disease.

fertility: the ability of soil to produce a large quantity of crops.

floodplain: the area of land beside a river or stream that is covered with water during a flood.

ice age: a period of time when the earth is very cold and lots of water in the oceans turns to ice.

immunity: natural protection from a disease.

incense: a substance that has a pleasant smell when burned.

irrigation: any system for watering the land to grow plants.

matchmaker: a person who arranges a marriage between two people.

merchandise: goods to be bought and sold.

midwife: a woman who helps other women give birth to their babies.

migration: movement from one place to another.

obsidian: a dark, natural glass formed by cooling lava.

reservation: land set aside by the U.S. government for specific Native American tribes to live on.

ritual: a system of special ceremonies.

sacrifice: to offer something to the gods as an act of worship; often involves killing an animal or a person.

slum: an overcrowded and unhygienic city district where very poor people live.

smallpox: a disease that causes a high fever and small bumps and that is passed on easily from person to person.

source: a written record that provides information.

tamales: ground meat rolled in cornmeal dough, then wrapped in corn husks and steamed.

tribute: a payment by one ruler or nation to another to show that it has been conquered.

MORE RESOURCES

WEBSITES:

http://ancientweb.org/explore/country/Mexico
  A brief history of the peoples of ancient Mexico, including the Aztecs.

http://library.thinkquest.org/27981/
  This website about all aspects of the ancient Aztecs includes a page about all the Aztec rulers and how they were related.

http://www.ancientscripts.com/aztec.html
  A well-illustrated web page about the signs and symbols in Aztec documents.

http://www.aztec-history.com/index.html
  A website full of details about all aspects of Aztec life and culture, including maps of the Aztec world.

http://www.aztecs.mrdonn.org/
  A site for younger children that includes aspects of everyday Aztec life.

http://www.mexicantextiles.com/index.html
  A website about the traditional clothing still made in Mexico with photos of the people who still wear these clothes and descriptions of modern Nahua villages.

http://www.mexicolore.co.uk/index.php
  A great website for children and schools about Mexico and the Aztecs. In the Aztec section, there are pages on Motecuhzoma, gods, health, music, the calendar, artifacts, significant animals, and much more.

http://www.native-languages.org/aztec-legends.htm
  Links to Aztec legends.

http://www.southamericanpictures.com/archaelogy-history/aztec/aztec-artifacts/aztec-artifacts-index.htm
  Photos of Aztec artifacts.

http://www.themexicotourist.com/2009/12/nahuatl/
  A web page about the Nahuatl language.

DVD:

The Aztec Empire. A & E Home Video, 2005.

BOOKS:

Apte, Sunita. *The Aztec Empire (True Books: Ancient Civilizations).* Children's Press, 2010.

Baquedano, Elizabeth, and Barry Clarke. *Aztec, Inca & Maya.* DK Children, 2011.

Callery, Sean. *The Dark History of the Aztec Empire.* Benchmark Books, 2010.

Clint, Marc. *Aztec Warriors (History's Greatest Warriors).* Bellwether Media, 2011.

Coulter, Laurie. *Ballplayers and Bonesetters: One Hundred Ancient Aztec and Maya Jobs You Might Have Adored or Abhorred (Jobs in History).* Annick Press, 2008.

Croy, Anita. *Solving the Mysteries of Aztec Cities (Digging into History).* Benchmark Books, 2009.

Doeden, Matt. *The Aztecs: Life in Tenochtitlan.* Millbrook Press, 2009.

Ganeri, Anita. *How the Aztecs Lived (Life in Ancient Times).* Gareth Stevens Publishing, 2010.

Green, Carl R. *Cortes: Conquering the Powerful Aztec Empire (Great Explorers of the World).* Enslow Publishers, 2010.

Green, Jen. *Aztecs (Flashback History).* PowerKids Press, 2009.

Green, Jen. *Hail! Aztecs (Hail! History).* Crabtree Publishing Company, 2010.

Hull, Robert. *The Aztec Empire (Exploring the Ancient World).* Gareth Stevens Publishing, 2010.

MacDonald, Fiona. *How to Be an Aztec Warrior.* National Geographic Children's Books, 2008.

Ollhoff, Jim. *Mayan and Aztec Mythology (The World of Mythology).* ABDO & Daughters, 2011.

Schomp, Virginia. *The Aztecs (Myths of the World).* Marshall Cavendish Children's Books, 2008.

THINGS TO THINK ABOUT AND DO

EVERY PICTURE TELLS A STORY

Make a codex. Fold a large sheet of white paper into a screen or fan.
Each fold will be a page of your codex. Now draw a story on your
codex, using picture symbols — no words — to tell your story.
You may make up your own picture symbols to use.

MEXICAN FLAG

Draw a picture of the flag of Mexico. Write down the meaning of
the Aztec symbols on the flag.

INVADERS! WHAT TO DO?

Each group of four to six people should pretend that they are
Motecuhzoma II and his advisors. Some strangers have been seen
entering your area. You know nothing about them. What should you
do about it? Remember, you are the most powerful and feared people
in Central America. Report back on your discussion and decisions.

YOU ARE THERE

Imagine that you are an Aztec boy or girl. Where do you think you
would fit in Aztec society? What do you think your life would be like?
How is it the same as or different from what it is now? What do your
parents do in Aztec society? What will you do when you grow up in
Tenochtitlán? Explain your thoughts in a brief essay.

INDEX

Adena culture 6
Alaska 4
American Indian Movement 9
arts and crafts 23, 25, 39
Asia 4
Aztlan 11

bark-paper paintings 26, 39
beliefs 10, 11, 25, 27, 28, 29, 30, 33–35, 37
Bering Strait 4

Cahokia, Illinois 6
calendars 25
Canada 4, 9
Chichimec people 12
children 22–23
chinampas 13
Cliff Palace, Mesa Verde 5
climate 4, 5
clothing 8, 20, 21, 23–24, 25, 36
codices (picture books) 8, 11, 12, 14, 16, 17, 18, 20, 21, 26, 27, 28
Cortés, Hernán 14, 15, 16, 17, 18, 25
crime 22
Cuauhtemoc, emperor 17
Cuitlahuac, emperor 15, 16, 17
Culhua people 12

dances 31, 33, 34
Day of the Dead 37

Diaz del Castillo, Bernal 18
Diego, Juan 35
diseases 8, 17, 18, 19
Duran, Fray 15

education 8, 9, 18, 19, 22–23
employment 32
Europeans 7–8, 10, 14–19, 26, 31, 32, 35

farming 5, 6, 9, 13, 20, 22, 24, 27, 31, 33, 34
feather work 14, 15, 20, 21, 22, 23, 25
fishing 5, 24, 33
food 22, 24, 33

games 24
gathering 5
gods 10–11, 12, 21, 25, 27, 28, 29, 33, 34, 35, 37
guns 7, 16

healers 34
Hopewell culture 6
horses 7, 16
housing 5, 6, 13, 23, 32–33
Huitzilopochtli, god 11, 27, 28
human sacrifice 12, 21, 24, 28, 29, 30
hunting 5, 24

ice ages 4

jewelry 14, 15, 23, 25

Lake Texcoco 7, 12, 13
language (Nahuatl) 8, 9, 10, 11,
    15, 19, 30, 31–32, 38

Malintzin (La Malinche) 15
markets 25, 39
marriage 8, 12, 19, 23, 30
Mexico City 8, 18, 19, 32, 37, 38
Mictlantecuhtli, god 37
migrations 4, 5, 7, 11, 12
missionaries 8
Motecuhzoma (Montezuma) II,
    emperor 13, 14, 15, 16, 17, 18

Nahua people 7, 8, 9, 10, 19,
    30–39
Nanaautzin, god 10–11
National Museum of
    Anthropology 38
National Palace 38

origin stories 10–11

Pipil people 31
poetry 25
pottery 23, 39
poverty 9, 32

Quetzalcoatl, god 10–11, 27, 29

Rivera, Diego 38, 39

sculpture 14, 21, 22, 24, 25, 27, 29
society 12, 19, 20–22
Spanish conquest 8, 10, 14–19
stories 10–11, 29

Tecuciztecatl, god 10–11
Templo Mayor Museum 38
Tenochtitlán 7, 8, 12, 13, 14, 15,
    17, 18, 21, 25, 26, 27, 30, 38, 39
Teotihuacán 6, 7
Texcoco, city-state 13, 16
Tezcatlipoca, god 10, 27
Tlacopán, city-state 13
Tlaloc, god 27
Toltec people 12, 25, 27
Tonantzin, goddess 35
Tonatiuh, god 27, 29
Totonac people 14, 39
trade 6, 7, 30
tributes 13–14, 18, 30
Triple Alliance 13–14

Virgin of Guadelupe 35
volador dance 34

warriors 8, 12, 13, 14, 15, 16, 17,
    21
weaving 22, 23–24, 36, 39

Xipe Totoc, god 29